MIND-STRETCHING MATH RIDDLES

MATH APPEAL

illustrated by
HARRY BRIGGS   by **GREG TANG**

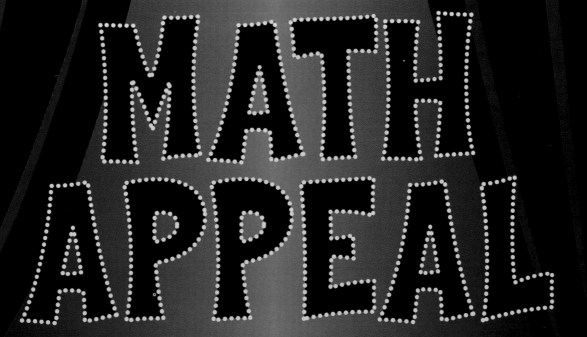

SCHOLASTIC PRESS • NEW YORK

A NOTE ABOUT *MATH APPEAL*

What's the best way to foster a love for learning? When we teach children to read, we share colorful picture books filled with exciting stories. When we teach science, we conduct lively, hands-on experiments that inspire curiosity and wonder. But what about math — is it possible to make math just as engaging and appealing to kids? The answer is yes! I believe language and art are the keys to making math more meaningful to children. Words and images have the power to communicate analytical reasoning and insight and at the same time connect math to a world of things — nature, science, art, and stories — that matter to kids.

I wrote *Math Appeal* for children ages 7–10, and like the other books in my series, *The Grapes of Math, Math For All Seasons,* and *The Best of Times,* my goal is to combine the teaching of problem-solving and arithmetic in a way that is challenging and fun for kids. I use poems and pictures to encourage clever, creative thinking, and I provide an answer key that teaches four important concepts: thinking out-of-the-box, finding strategic sums, using subtraction to add, and simplifying through patterns and symmetries. I encourage kids to discover different ways of solving each problem and to decide for themselves which approach works best.

In writing books for children, I hope to begin laying the foundation for higher math skills and a life-long love of math. I'd like to show kids firsthand the power of clear, common-sense thinking and help them gain the confidence to know they can be good at math. I hope you find *Math Appeal* to be entertaining and enlightening, and a book you'll want to share with a child. Enjoy!

Greg Tang

With love to Katie,
my inspiration
— G. T.

To James Briggs,
my dad
— H. B.

SQUARE DEAL

My kite flies high, my kite flies free,
My kite just landed in a tree!

I was busy counting squares,
Now my kite is stuck up there.

How many squares? Let me see,
It's best to add diagonally!

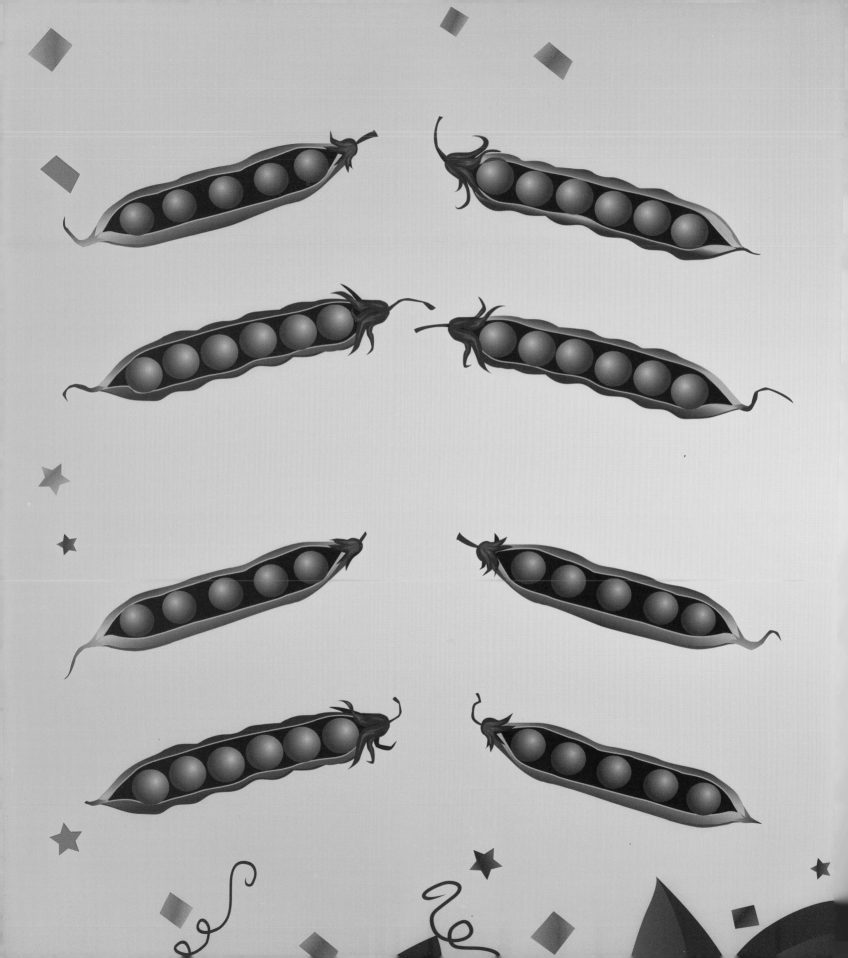

BOSTON PEA PARTY

A pea would find it rather odd,
To be alone inside a pod.

They like to hang out with their friends,
For them the party never ends!

Can you count up all the peas?
With 11's it's a breeze!

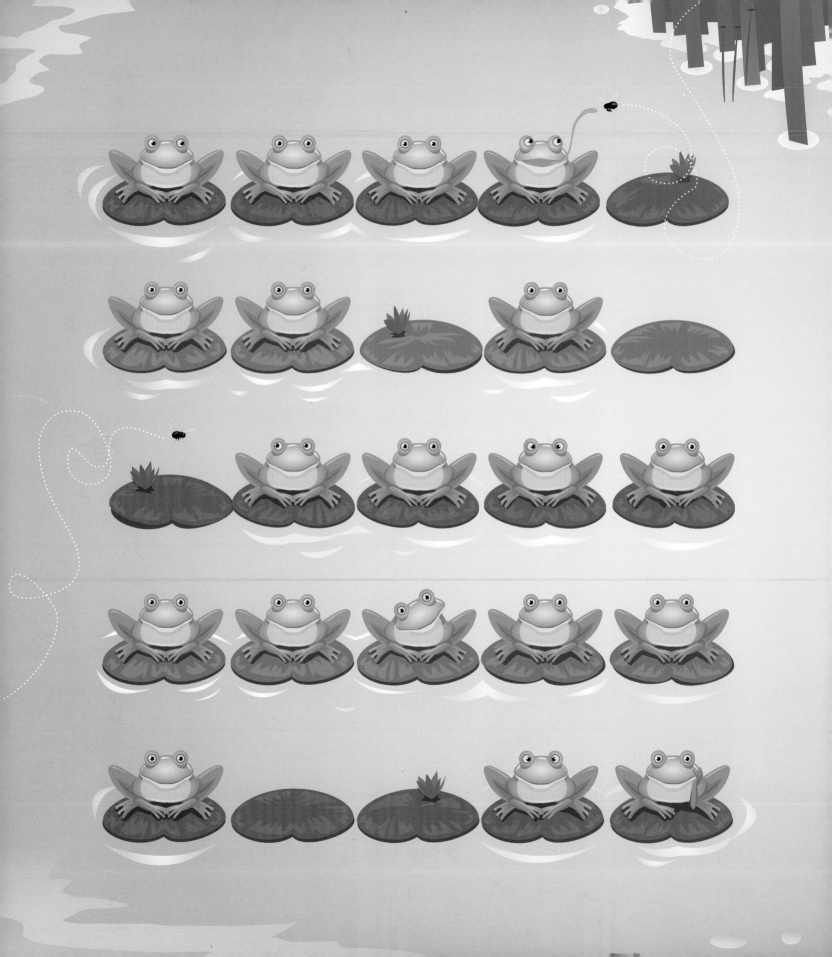

FROG-GONE!

It's roll call at the local bog,
Can you count each friendly frog?

Some are sitting — calm and pleasant,
Some are swimming — they're not present.

Here's a tip to help you add,
Don't ignore a lily pad!

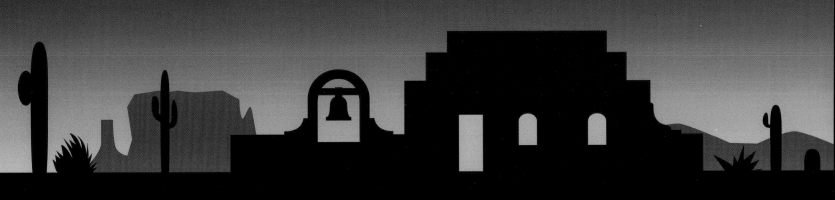

RED HOT CHILI PEPPERS

Chilis take a long siesta,
Then head out for a fiesta.

Noon's the time for feeling lazy,
Night's the time for going crazy!

How many peppers on the town?
Don't count up or even down.

Group the chilis in the square,
Add the rest and you'll be there!

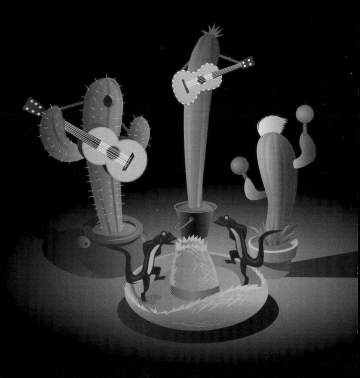

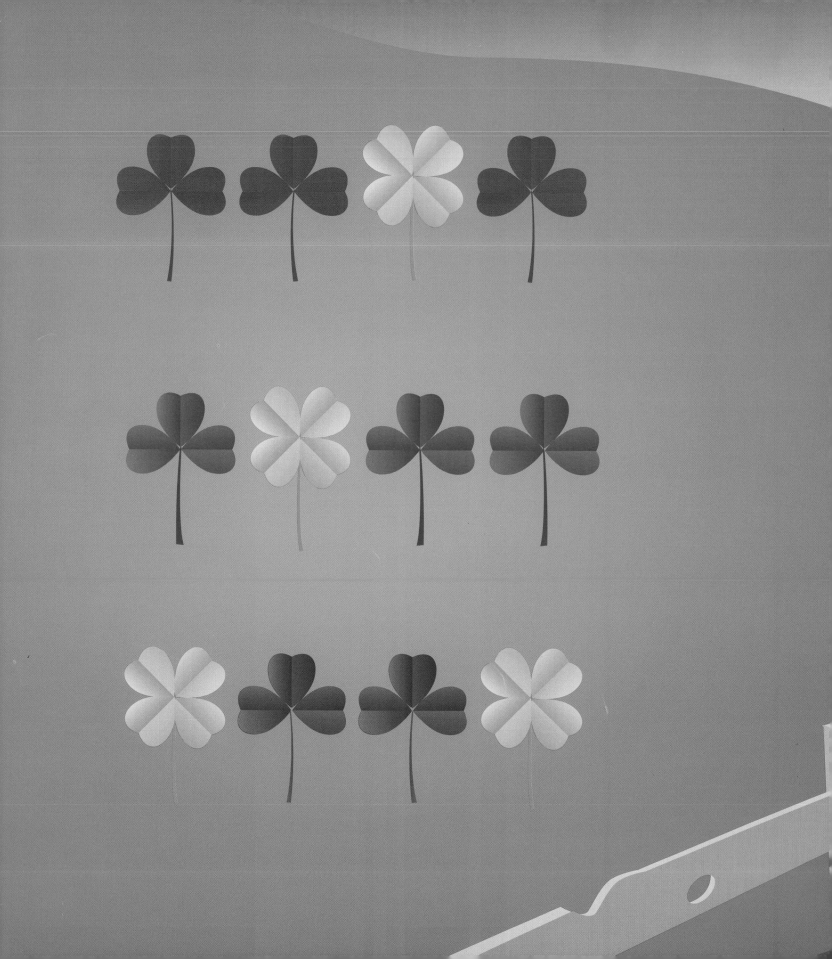

LUCKY CLOVERS

There among the blades of grass,
I came across a clover mass.

Some had 4 leaves, some had 3,
How many total do you see?

Instead of counting row by row,
Why not add the leaves below!

SPELLBOUND

High up in the autumn sky,
Noisy geese are flying by.

They somehow know to make a V,
Instead of flying randomly!

How many geese are in this scene?
Try to focus on 15!

AIR SHOW *Today*

SPELL

ROCK STARS

With little suction cups for feet,
Starfish look for food to eat.

You can find them holding tight,
To rocky bottoms out of sight.

How many starfish are in view?
This is all you have to do.

Instead of counting one by one,
Just subtract and you'll be done!

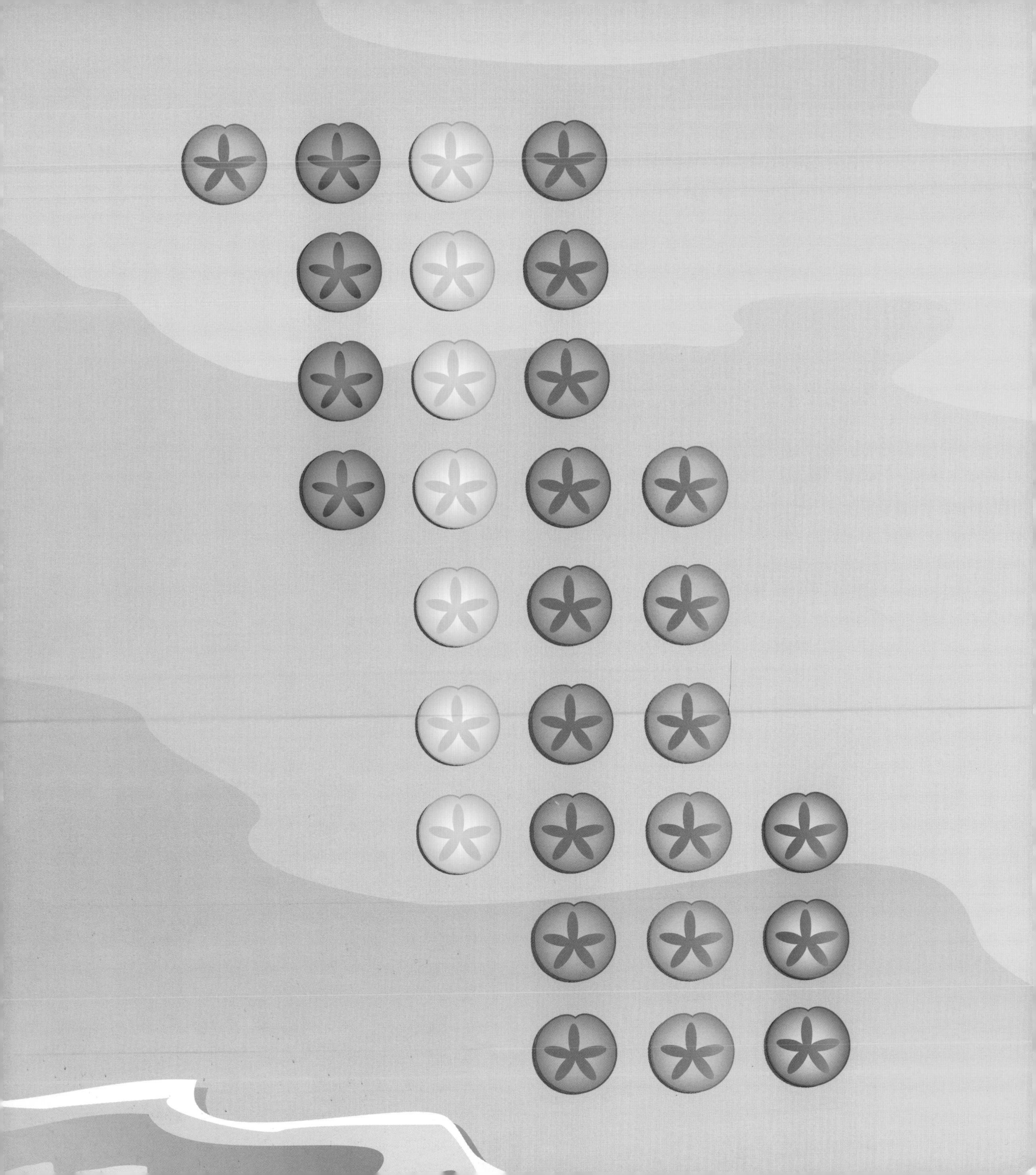

ESTATE SALE

To buy a castle really grand,
You'll need some money made of sand.

But on the beach you're never poor,
Just look around and find some more!

How many dollars can you spot?
Hurry quick — it's getting hot.

Try to make a group of 10,
Then find this pattern once again!

DEW THE MATH

The day began all damp and gray,
With many raindrops in the way.

But once the clouds began to clear,
A misty rainbow did appear.

Can you count the drops of dew?
Try to see a way that's new.

When counting drops come rain or shine,
A curve is better than a line!

LADiES-iN-WAiTiNG

Ladybugs forward, please advance.
Join us in the ladybug dance!

Bow to your partners one and all,
How many dots in the old dance hall?

Here's a clue we'd like to share,
To count them fast just find a pair!

Spring Dance

SEE-HORSE STAMPEDE

Hi-ho Silver, away we go!
These small creatures swim, you know.

Try to catch them — they'll stampede,
And ride away at breakneck speed.

How many horses in the sea?
Don't just count, think cleverly.

It may be wise to use this tack,
Add them all and then subtract!

O.K. CORAL

FLOWERY ATTIRE

Flowers try to look their best,
They're always very smartly dressed.

They add such color to a scene,
While other plants wear only green.

How many petals do you see?
It helps to think of symmetry.

Instead of counting every one,
Double twice and you'll be done!

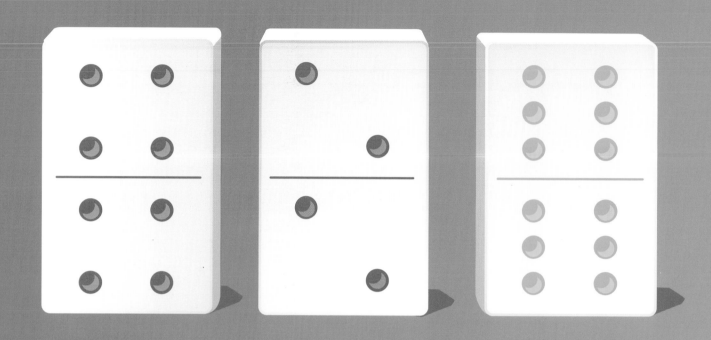

DOMi-NOSE

A domino stands straight and tall,
Always ready for a fall.

A little push and there it goes —
Falling right down on its nose!

Can you count the dots you see?
Try to think horizontally!

PICK
YOUR OWN

ISAAC'S APPLE

When Newton sat beneath this tree,
He didn't know of gravity.

Then an apple shiny red,
Tumbled down and hit his head!

How many apples are in sight?
Here's a way that's really bright.

If you want to count them fast,
Keep adding first rows to the last!

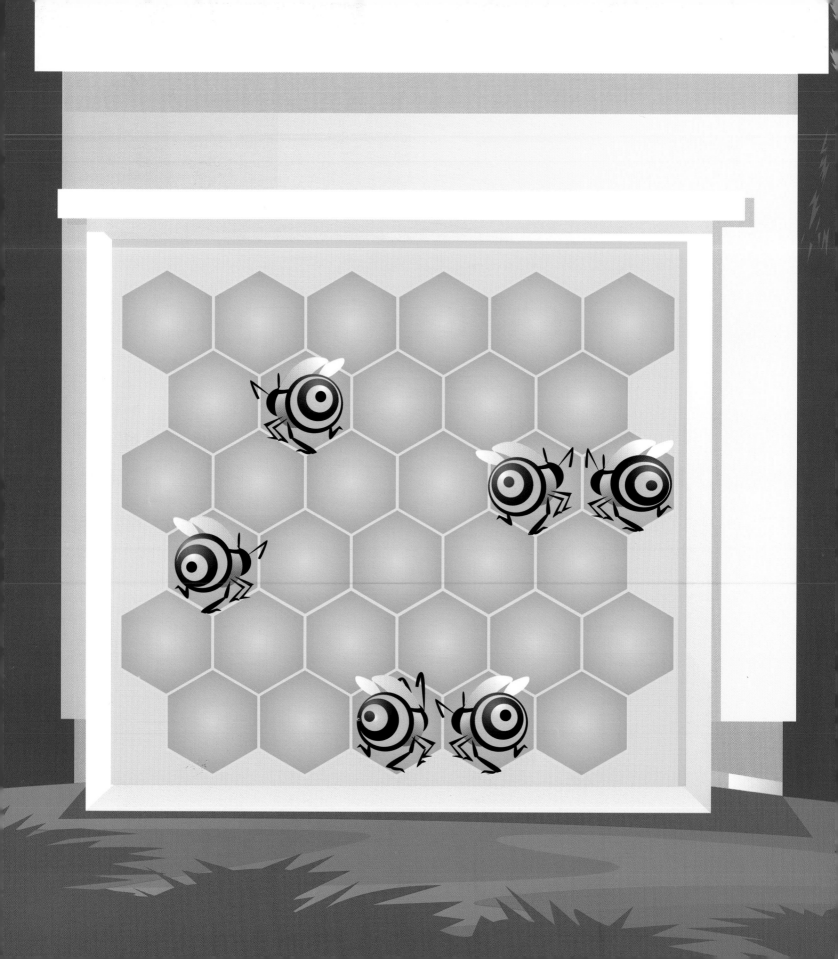

HOME SWEET COMB

A hive is what a bee calls home.
It's also called a honeycomb!

The bees store honey, sticky sweet,
In lots of little cells so neat.

Can you count each empty cell?
Here's a way that works quite well.

Pair the rows and get the sum,
Subtract the bees and you'll be done!

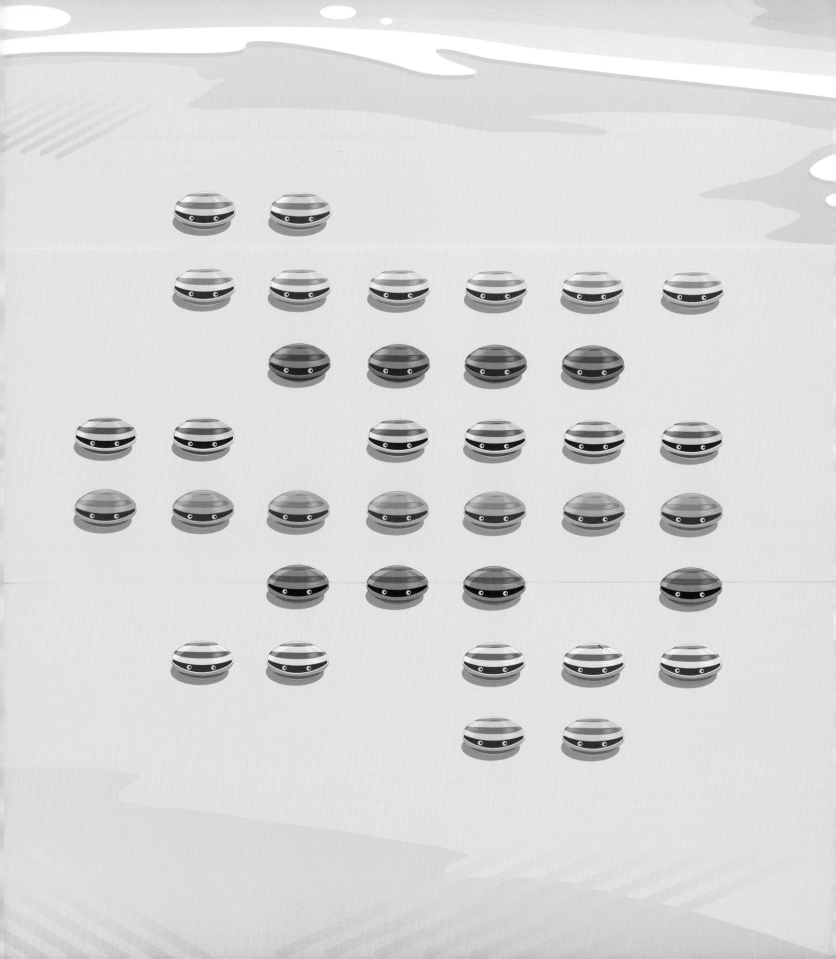

RUDE A-RAKE-NING

The clams were happy as can be,
All were sleeping restfully.

Then they felt the dreaded rake —
How many clams are now awake?

It helps to move the clams around,
At least until a pattern is found!

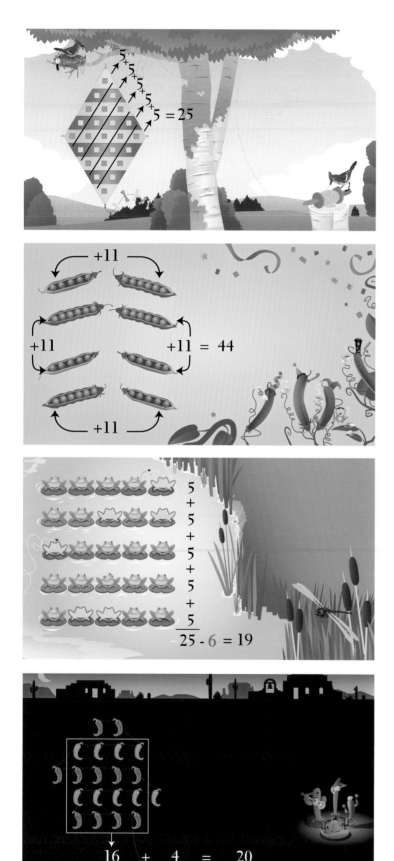

ANSWERS

SQUARE DEAL

Instead of seeing the squares in rows, look along the diagonal and you will see 5 groups of 5 squares, or 25 squares.

$5 + 5 + 5 + 5 + 5 = 25$

BOSTON PEA PARTY

When possible, add numbers that have easy sums. The pea pods can be matched to create 4 pairs that each total 11, so there are 44 peas altogether.

$11 + 11 + 11 + 11 = 44$

FROG-GONE!

First imagine a frog on each of the 6 empty lily pads. Then there are 5 rows of 5 frogs, or 25 frogs. Now subtract the imaginary frogs and you are left with 19 frogs.

$25 - 6 = 19$

RED HOT CHILI PEPPERS

Find a square consisting of 4 rows of 4 peppers, or 16 peppers. Add the remaining peppers to get 20 peppers altogether.

$16 + 1 + 2 + 1 = 20$

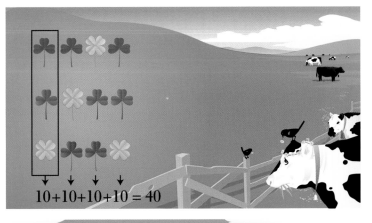

LUCKY CLOVERS

Rather than adding leaves across each row, add down along each column. Since each column has 10 leaves, there are 40 leaves altogether.

$10 + 10 + 10 + 10 = 40$

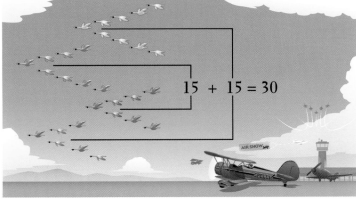

SPELLBOUND

When possible, add numbers that have easy sums. The geese can be matched to create 2 pairs that each total 15, so there are 30 geese altogether.

$15 + 15 = 30$

ROCK STARS

First imagine 6 starfish where they seem to be missing. Then there are 6 rows of 6 starfish, or 36 starfish. Now subtract the imaginary starfish, and you are left with 30 starfish.

$36 - 6 = 30$

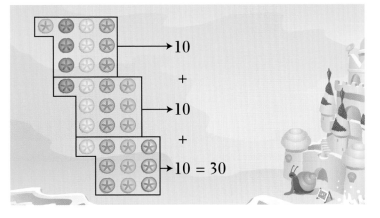

ESTATE SALE

Make a group of 10 sand dollars consisting of those in the top 3 rows. Notice that this pattern repeats itself twice below, so there are 30 sand dollars altogether.

$10 + 10 + 10 = 30$

DEW THE MATH

Instead of seeing 5 straight lines each with 7 drops, look across the rainbow to see 5 drops in each color. There are 35 drops altogether.

$$5 + 5 + 5 + 5 + 5 + 5 + 5 = 35$$

LADIES-IN-WAITING

When possible, add numbers that have easy sums. The ladybugs can be matched to create 4 pairs that each total 10, so there are 40 dots altogether.

$$10 + 10 + 10 + 10 = 40$$

SEE-HORSE STAMPEDE

First count all 36 creatures by adding along the diagonal. Now subtract the 5 scallops and starfish, and you are left with 31 sea horses.

$$36 - 5 = 31$$

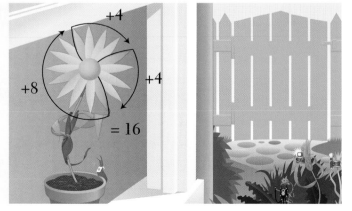

FLOWERY ATTIRE

Since the flower is symmetrical and can be divided evenly into 4 sections, just count 4 petals and double once to get half the petals, then double twice to get all the petals. There are 16 petals all together.

$$4 + 4 + 8 = 16$$

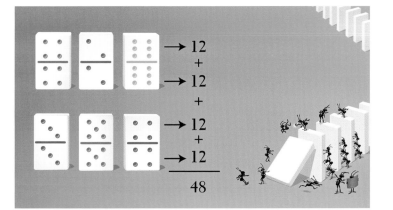

DOMI-NOSE

Rather than adding the pairs of dots on each domino, notice that each row has 12 dots. Since there are 4 rows, there are 48 dots altogether.

$12 + 12 + 12 + 12 = 48$

ISAAC'S APPLE

When adding consecutive numbers, it is helpful to pair the first and last numbers, the second and second-to-last numbers, and so on. All the pairs will have the same total! Here, the sum of each of the 3 pairs is 11, so there are 33 apples altogether.

$11 + 11 + 11 = 33$

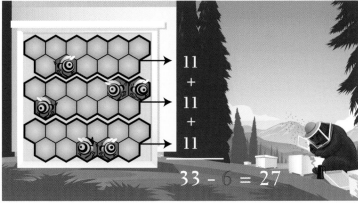

HOME SWEET COMB

First count all the cells by pairing the rows. Each pair has 11 cells, so there are 33 cells altogether. Now subtract the 6 cells with bees, and you are left with 27 empty cells.

$33 - 6 = 27$

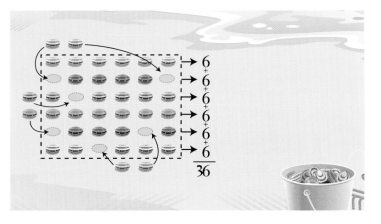

RUDE A-RAKE-NING

You can move 6 clams to form a rectangle with 6 rows of 6 clams. There are 36 clams altogether.

$6 + 6 + 6 + 6 + 6 + 6 = 36$

ACKNOWLEDGMENTS

Special thanks to Jean Feiwel, Liz Szabla, David Caplan,
Stephanie Luck, Daniel Narahara, and Jeffrey Wheeler

Library of Congress Cataloging-in-Publication Data
Tang, Greg.
Math appeal / by Greg Tang; illustrated by Harry Briggs.-- 1st ed.   p.   cm.
Summary: Rhyming anecdotes present opportunities
for simple math activities and hints for solving.
1. Mathematics--Juvenile literature. [1. Mathematics.
2. Mathematical recreations.] I. Briggs, Harry, ill. II. Title.
QA40.5 .T36 2003   510--dc21   2002005354
ISBN 0-439-21046-1
10 9 8 7 6 5 4 3 2 1   03 04 05 06 07

Printed in Mexico   49
First edition, February 2003
The text type was set in Electra LH Bold.
The display type was set in Coop Heavy.
Harry Briggs's artwork was created on the computer.
For more information about Greg Tang and his books,
visit www.gregtang.com. Book design by Greg Tang.